THREE-*in*-ONE

GOD *the* FATHER — GOD *the* SON — GOD *the* SPIRIT
and
GOD'S CHILDREN

CAPERNAUM VERSION

1941
PUBLISHING™

THREE-IN-ONE: Capernaum Version
© 2022 Young Life Discipleship

Publisher: 1941 Publishing™ (a division of Young Life Discipleship)
Young Life, P.O. Box 540, Colorado Springs, CO 80901
discipleship.younglife.org
discipleship@sc.younglife.org

Printed in the United States of America

Content Development: Young Life Discipleship Field Elders and Advisors
Writer: Crystal Kirgiss
Capernaum Collaborator and Writer: Sara Webb
Copy Editors: Sara Webb, Amira Bartley, Suzanne Williams
Cover Design, Layout: Matt Wallace
Capernaum Version Adaptations: Isaac Watkins

The publication and printing of this book was made possible by a generous grant from the Young Life Store (younglifestore.com).

Proceeds from sales of this book will be used to help fund future 1941 Publishing discipleship projects.

Image p 9: detail of the Flammarion woodcut, unknown artist and date, public domain.
Image p 17: detail of Jesus washing disciples' feet, unknown artist and date,. Expanded license image 19009130 from Vectorstock.
Image p 25: detail of Pentecost woodcut, unknown artist and date, public domain.
Image p 33: detail of prodigal son's return, unknown artist and date. Commercial license image 187864 from FCIT.

younglife.
Discipleship

CONTENTS

THREE-in-ONE.

GOD IS OFTEN DESCRIBED AS THREE-IN-ONE BECAUSE HE IS
THE FATHER,
AND ALSO THE SON,
AND ALSO THE HOLY SPIRIT.

     THAT IS A MYSTERY TO HUMAN MINDS.

     BUT GOD IS BIGGER THAN HUMAN MINDS.

THE WORLD HAS MANY IDEAS ABOUT WHAT GOD IS LIKE, WHO JESUS IS,
AND WHAT THE SPIRIT DOES. MOST OF THOSE IDEAS ARE WRONG. SOME
ARE JUST SILLY. OTHERS ARE DANGEROUS.

THE BEST PLACE TO LEARN THE TRUTH ABOUT GOD IS THE BIBLE. IT TELLS
US WHO GOD IS, WHAT HE IS LIKE, WHY HE CARES ABOUT THE WORLD, AND
HOW HE FEELS ABOUT PEOPLE.

THE BIBLE IS A VERY OLD BOOK. BUT IT TELLS A TIMELESS STORY. IT STILL
HAS TRUTH AND WISDOM FOR ALL PEOPLE, NO MATTER WHERE OR WHEN
THEY LIVE.

GOD IS A MYSTERY. BUT WE CAN KNOW HIM.

GOD IS SUPERNATURAL. BUT WE CAN EXPERIENCE HIM.

GOD IS INFINITE. BUT HE MEETS WITH US HERE AND NOW.

GOD IS GOD. BUT HE LOVES HUMANS. VERY MUCH.

GOD IS OUR FATHER, SAVIOR, AND LORD. WE ARE HIS CHILDREN.

NO TRUTH IS MORE IMPORTANT THAN THAT. SO LET'S READ GOD'S WORD
TO LEARN ABOUT HIM, HIS PLANS. AND HIS PEOPLE.

AMEN!

ABOUT THIS BOOK

EACH DEVO INCLUDES THESE THINGS ON THE LEFT PAGE.

◊ SOMETHING TO READ

    THIS WILL HELP YOU START THINKING AND LEARNING.

◊ BIBLE VERSES TO READ OR LISTEN TO

    THIS IS WHAT GOD WANTS TO TEACH US.

◊ FANCY SUN

    HERE, WRITE SOMETHING YOU WILL THINK ABOUT, LEARN,
    PRAY ABOUT, OR DO THAT DAY.

EACH DEVO INCLUDES THESE THINGS ON THE RIGHT PAGE.

◊ "THINK ABOUT"

    THESE ARE QUESTIONS THAT WILL HELP YOU THINK ABOUT
    THE BIBLE VERSES. IF YOU LIKE TO READ YOUR BIBLE IN NEW
    WAYS TO LEARN EVEN MORE THINGS, LOOK AT THE NEXT PAGE
    FOR SOME IDEAS ABOUT THAT.

◊ P.S.

    SOME PEOPLE ADD A P.S. TO THE END OF THEIR LETTERS. IT
    MEANS THEY HAVE ONE MORE THING THEY WANT TO WRITE.
    THE P.S HAS MORE BIBLE VERSES THAT ARE CONNECTED TO
    WHAT YOU ARE READING AND LEARNING THAT DAY. READ
    THEM IF YOU WANT TO.

◊ FANCY MOON

    HERE, WRITE ABOUT SOMETHING GOD SHOWED YOU OR TAUGHT YOU
    OR DID FOR YOU THAT DAY. IT'S GOOD TO REMEMBER THOSE THINGS!

ABOUT READING THE BIBLE

SOME MORE WAYS TO READ & LEARN GOD'S WORD:

◊ HEAR IT — LISTEN TO SOMEONE ELSE READ IT. DON'T FOLLOW
ALONG IN YOUR BIBLE. JUST LISTEN.

◊ COPY IT — SIMPLY CHOOSE ONE OR SOME VERSES TO COPY OUT IN A
JOURNAL. THIS REQUIRES YOU TO SLOW DOWN. SLOWING DOWN
HELPS YOU NOTICE THINGS OFTEN MISSED WHEN READING QUICKLY.

◊ PRAY IT — FOR EXAMPLE: "HE WAS HANDED OVER TO DIE BECAUSE
OF OUR SINS" CAN BE PRAYED LIKE THIS: "THANK YOU FOR DYING
FOR MY SINS." "DON'T COPY THE BEHAVIORS AND CUSTOMS OF THIS
WORLD" CAN BE PRAYED LIKE THIS: "LORD, HELP ME TO NOT COPY THE
WAYS OF THIS WORLD."

◊ MARK IT — AS YOU READ, LOOK FOR THE THEMES LISTED BELOW
(AND ANY OTHERS YOU WANT TO INCLUDE). DRAW THE RELEVANT
ICON IN THE MARGIN OF YOUR BIBLE. OVER TIME, YOU'LL GROW INTO
BEING A MORE THOUGHTFUL READER, AND YOU'LL BE ABLE TO QUICKLY
AND EASILY FIND AND TRACE THESE THEMES.

GOD'S LOVE FOR US   KING / LORD / KINGDOM OF GOD

OUR LOVE FOR GOD   FORGIVENESS / WASHED CLEAN

OUR LOVE FOR OTHERS   SIN / DISOBEDIENCE / OLD LIFE

CROSS / CRUCIFIXION   OBEDIENCE / NEW LIFE

RESURRECTION   SPIRITUAL FRUIT

REPENTANCE   ABIDE / CHRIST IN YOU

TRUST / BELIEVE   HOLY SPIRIT

WISDOM   PRAYER

JOY   LIGHT

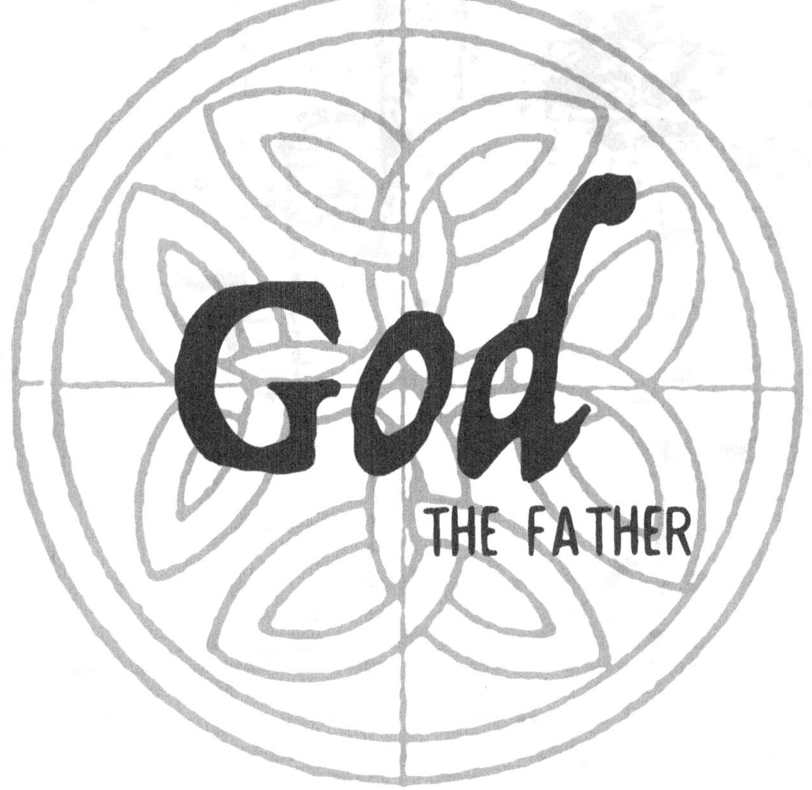

God

THE FATHER

THE FAITHFUL LOVE OF THE LORD NEVER ENDS! HIS MERCIES NEVER CEASE.
GREAT IS HIS FAITHFULNESS.
HIS MERCIES BEGIN AFRESH EACH MORNING.

(LAMENTATIONS 3:22–23)

God THE FATHER
In the beginning

How does your Bible start? (You could look at the first verse right now if you want to.)

Does it say, "This is a very great book! God is very great!"
Does it say, "This is a very big book! God is very big!"
Does it say, "This is a very important book! God is very important!"

Those things are true. But that's not how the Bible starts, does it?
It starts like this:

> *In the beginning* (this is such a good way to start a story, isn't it?)
> *God created the heavens and the earth.*

In the beginning means God is the first thing of all things.
God created means God is where all things come from.
Heaven and earth means God is in charge of everything, everywhere.

The very first thing the Bible tells us about God is that he makes things.
He knows how to take something that doesn't have any shape or meaning or purpose or beauty and turn it into something that does.

It is so nice to know God makes everything, including you and me.

READ OR LISTEN: Genesis 1, Isaiah 40:12-31

Today, we will ...

THINK ABOUT...

What is something you like to make?

What part of God's creation do you love most? Why?

What did you learn about God today?

 Today, God did ...

 *devo* **2**   # God THE FATHER
I AM

Did you know that God has a name? Did you know that his name isn't God? It's okay if you think that's his name, and it's okay to keep calling him "God." You call your mom and dad "Mom" and "Dad." But that's not their real name.

When people first started knowing about God, they thought that his name was too special to speak out loud. So they called him God and Lord instead.

But God did tell his real name to his people. The first person he told was a man named Moses. He said his name was "I AM." That's an odd name, isn't it? It means "I am who I have always been and who I will always be. I never change. I have always existed. I am ME!"

God's personal name is Yahweh. It's pronounced like this: YA'-way. It looks like this in the old language:

יהוה

In the old language, words go opposite, from right to left. The letters in this word are yod (י) hay (ה) vav (ו) hay (ה) . When your Bible has the word LORD with all capital letters, that means Yahweh. You can still read it as LORD, but now you know that it means something even more than that. You know God's name!

READ OR LISTEN: Exodus 3:1-17

 *Today, we will ...*

THINK ABOUT...

Who do you call by their real name? Who do you not call by their real name?

Why do you think God wanted Moses (and you!) to know his real name?

What did you learn about God today?

Try to write God's name with the old letters.

Today, God did ...

God THE FATHER
Worthy of Praise

It's hard to explain how BIG God is.

It's hard to describe how AMAZING God is.

It's hard to talk about how FANTASTIC God is.

Sometimes you can only understand God by singing a song.

The Bible has a whole collection of songs about God. It's called the book of Psalms because "psalm" was the word for song or poem in the old language. (The letter "p" is silent. Say **salm**.)

When we praise something, it's like yelling a giant "YES!!!!" because the thing is so awesome and great and wonderful.

When we praise God with our words or our singing or our actions or our prayers, it's like yelling a giant "YES" about God. YES I believe in you. YES I love you. YES I know you made everything. YES I know you love me. YES I know you are the only real God. YES I know that you are powerful and strong.

Let's praise God with a giant YES every day.

READ OR LISTEN: Psalm 103:1-22

Today, we will ...

THINK ABOUT...

How do you praise God with your words?

How do you praise God with your actions?

How else do you like to praise God?

What did you learn about God today?

Praise God by singing a song or drawing a picture

Today, God did ...

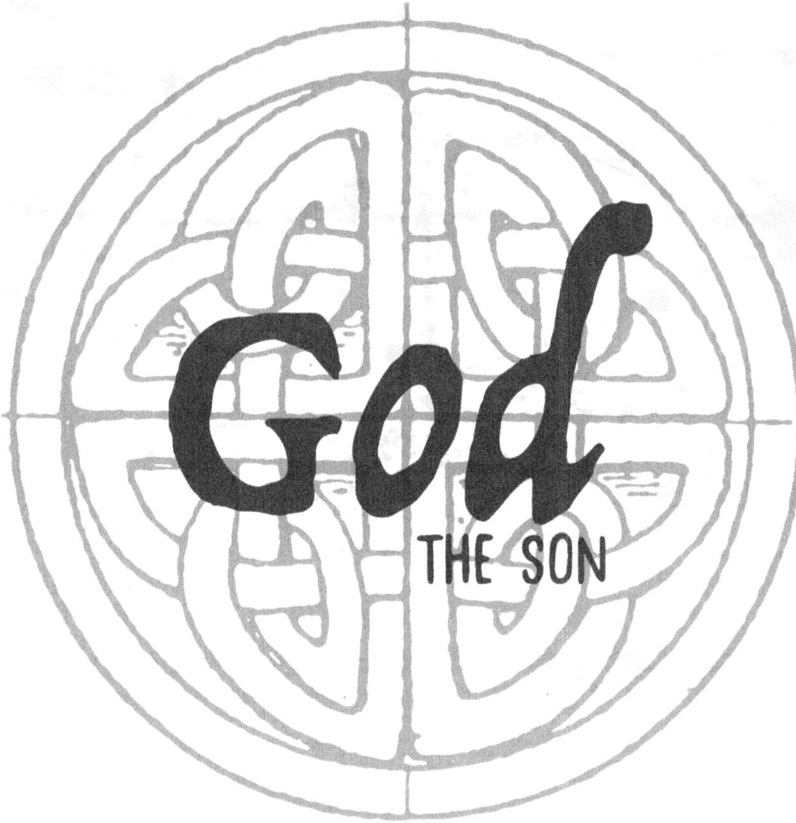

God
THE SON

I AM THE WAY, THE TRUTH, AND THE LIFE.
NO ONE CAN COME TO THE FATHER
EXCEPT THROUGH ME. —JESUS

JOHN 14:6

God THE SON
In the beginning

Do you remember the very first words of the Bible we read a few days ago? They weren't, "Once upon a time," even though many books start that way.

The Bible starts like this: "In the beginning God created..." (From Genesis 1)

The verses today start almost exactly the same way? "In the beginning was the Word..." (From John 1)

Do you see what's the same? Do you see what's different?

In Genesis, the verses are about God. In John (the book you're going to read from today) the verses are about someone called the Word. That's a funny name for a person. Here, "the Word" means Jesus.

So you could rewrite the John verse like this: "In the beginning **Jesus** ..."
And the Genesis verse is like this: "In the beginning **God** ..."

Look carefully - do you see the matching pairs?

Yes! Jesus was in the beginning, and God was in the beginning because
JESUS IS GOD!

It's okay if you don't understand it. You only have to believe it.

READ OR LISTEN: John 1:1-18

Today, we will ...

THINK ABOUT...

How do some of your favorite books, stories, and movies start?

Why do you think it's important to know that Jesus IS God?

What did you learn about God and Jesus from the verses you read?

Today, God did ...

God THE SON
I AM

Do you remember when God called himself **I AM** to a man named Moses? (We talked about that in devo 2.)

Jesus said the same thing about himself. He spoke in pictures about himself, like this:

> **I am** the light of the world.
> **I am** the bread of life.
> **I am** the good shepherd.
> **I am** the way, the truth, and the life.
> **I am** the door.

Then he said, "**I AM**," just like God did, because Jesus is God.

> "**I AM** who I have always been
> and who I am right now,
> and who I will always be.
> **I AM**!"

When Jesus said, "I am the bread of life," he didn't mean he was actually a loaf of bread or a piece of bread. He meant that he feeds our soul and makes it grow and keeps it healthy, just like bread does for our body.

READ OR LISTEN: John 6:5-15, John 6:22-35

Today, we will ...

THINK ABOUT...

What are some "I am" statements about you?
(Like: I am strong. I am creative. I am musical. I am quiet.)

How is Jesus like bread?

What did you learn about Jesus today?

P.S. SIX OTHER I AM STATEMENTS IN JOHN'S GOSPEL ACCOUNT: 8:12 . 10:9 . 10:11 . 11:25 . 14:6 . 15:1

 *Today, God did ...*

God THE SON
In the beginning

Jesus is God. He came to earth and became human just like us. He was born a tiny baby, like every other person. First he was a baby, then he was a kid, then a boy, then a young man, then a man. He grew up just like all people do. Just imagine: Jesus, who was there with God creating the whole world, had to learn how to walk, how to talk, how to read, how to feed himself, and how to tie his sandals onto his feet.

Jesus is the most important person who ever lived. He could have walked around saying, "Look at me! I'm the most important person who ever lived! I'm the King! Do what I say! Right now!!" Powerful people are sometimes pushy or bossy or proud. Jesus was powerful - but he was also humble and obedient, so he treated people with kindness, goodness, and love. When he became a human being, Jesus willingly humbled himself in order to be with us and show us God's love.

Today you'll read about Jesus both being God and also obeying God. (That's mysterious, isn't it?) You'll read about Jesus being humble as a human and also being lifted up to the place of highest honor. Those things might sound opposite, but with Jesus they can both be true. You'll read about Jesus who is love and also God. You'll read about Jesus who is our Savior and also King.

We are told to learn from Jesus and live like Jesus. If Jesus was humble and thought of other people before himself, then we should do the same because we love him and we follow him.

READ OR LISTEN: Philippians 2:6-11

Today, we will ...

THINK ABOUT...

Write or draw the words from the verse that describe who Jesus is.

How was Jesus humble? How can we be more like Jesus?
Reminder: Being humble is thinking about others more than ourselves.

What did you learn about Jesus today?

P.S.

REVELATION 5 IS A VISION OF BOTH THE HUMBLE AND REIGNING JESUS.

Today, God did . . .

God
THE SPIRIT

FOR THE LORD IS THE SPIRIT,
AND WHEREVER THE SPIRIT OF THE LORD IS,
THERE IS FREEDOM.

2 CORINTHIANS 3:17

God THE SPIRIT
In the beginning

God the Father was there when everything was created. (You read about that in Genesis 1.)

God the Son, Jesus, was there when everything was created. (You read about that in John 1.)

God the Spirit was there when everything was created, too. (You also read about that in Genesis 1, but you might not remember.) It could not be any other way since they are three-in-one.

Before anything was created, God the Spirit was flying over the surface of the deep waters (Gen. 1:2). Then God the Father, Son and Spirit created the heavens and the earth together as one. Everything we see! They were all three there when everything was created.

Maybe God the Spirit (sometimes we call him the Holy Spirit) is a new idea for you. But we talk about God the Spirit without even knowing it. Have you ever said, "I have God in my heart"? Or said, "God is in my life"? That is God the Spirit. God the Spirit is always with us – in our hearts and with us every day of our lives.

Here's something special to know: the word for "Spirit" in the old language is "breath." That's one way you could try to understand God the Spirit: it is the breath of God that breathes into us.

READ OR LISTEN: John 14:15-31

Today, we will …

THINK ABOUT...

Draw what you think God the Spirit looks like – is the Spirit something you can see or is it invisible?

Jesus describes God the Spirit as a friend. Who is your best friend and what makes them a good friend?

What did you learn about God the Spirit today?

Today, God did ...

God THE SPIRIT
comforter and Guide

Understanding the three-in-one God is hard. It is like a mystery our heads can't solve.

God the Father: we know and understand what a Father is.

God the Son: we know what it means to be human, and we understand what a son is.

God the Spirit: this is much harder to understand. It's like wind: you can't see the wind, but you can feel it. You can't catch it in your hands, but you can feel it on your face.

You can't see the Spirit or hold it in your hands, but you can feel it inside of you, filling your heart with God's love.

One way to begin understanding God the Spirit is to remember the Spirit is the presence of God that fills our lives and connects us to each other. God's Spirit is the part of God that lives inside his children.

God the Spirit is with us and in our hearts.

READ OR LISTEN: Acts 1:8, 2 Corinthians 1:22, Ephesians 1:13-14

Today, we will ...

THINK ABOUT...

When God the Spirit lives in our heart, we want to tell others about God.
Who are your favorite people to tell about the God that lives in your heart?

When God the Spirit lives in us we are confident we belong.
What does it mean to belong? What does it mean to belong to God?

What have you learned about God the Spirit today?

 Today, God did ...

God THE SPIRIT
Life Transformer

One thing we know for sure about God the Spirit, he works in our lives, slowly shaping and changing us from the inside out into the person he wants us to become.

It is not always easy. It is not always fast. It is sometimes like a powerful back-and-forth tug-of-war in your heart. One side says, "I want, I deserve, I will, I am in charge". The other side says, "God loves, God says, God is God.".

Sometimes we get stuck with bad thoughts or a grumpy attitude and we have to remember that God the Spirit that lives in you is greater than any power. So the back-and-forth and tug-of-war is real, but it can be won with the Spirit's help.

God the Spirit has the power to change your thoughts, your attitudes, and your actions if you allow him to. When our lives are changed by God the Spirit, we live more like Jesus and love more like Jesus. We are more loving, joyful, kind, patient, peaceful, gentle, faithful, and self-controlled.

Sometimes the Bible calls that "fruit" because it grows out of a healthy life, just like real fruit grows out of a healthy tree.

READ OR LISTEN: Galatians 5:16-26

Today, we will ...

THINK ABOUT...

Write or draw the words that are good actions and attitudes from God (these verses call them fruit.)

What kind of "fruit" (good actions/attitudes) is the Spirit growing in you?

How do you use good fruit to show Jesus to other people?

What did you learn about God's Spirit today?

Today, God did ...

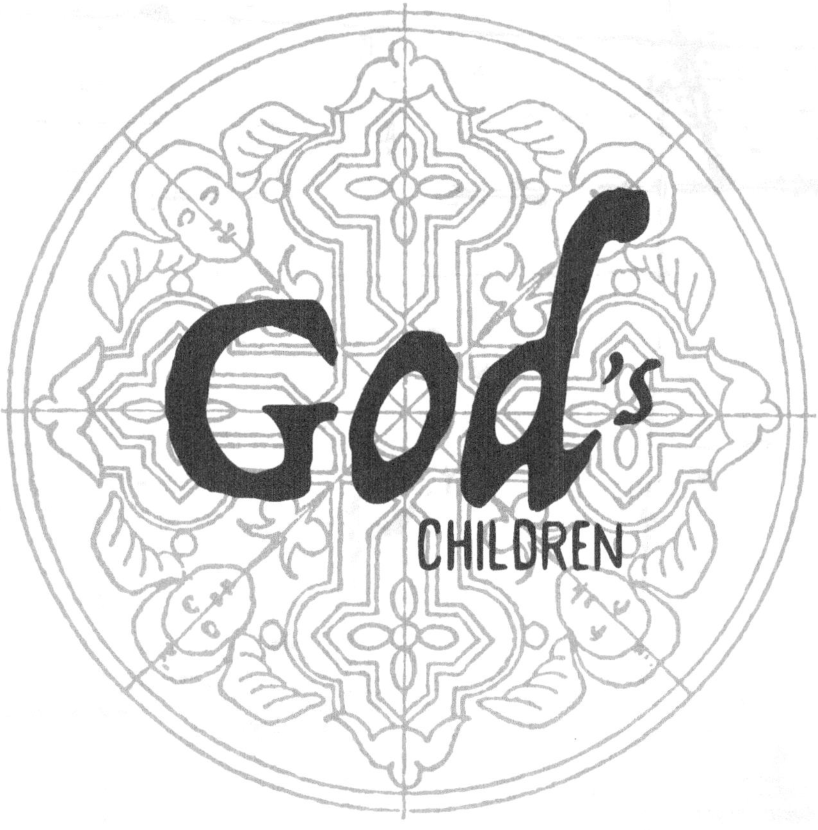

God's CHILDREN

BUT TO ALL WHO BELIEVED HIM AND ACCEPTED HIM,
HE GAVE THE RIGHT TO BECOME CHILDREN OF GOD.

JOHN 1:12

God's CHILDREN
In the beginning

The first three words of the Bible are "In the beginning."

Genesis 1 and 2 tell the story of God creating everything. God created the sun. The moon. The stars. God created every tree, animal and bug. God created everything we can see and everything we can't see.

And most wonderful of all, God created YOU. God created you on purpose and because He wanted YOU to be in this world. How incredible is God?! And how incredible does that make YOU?!

There is a fancy Latin pair of words – **_imago Dei_** – that mean 'Image of God'.

YOU were created in the imago Dei – the image of God.

To be created in God's image means that you belong! God knows how many hairs are on your head. God knows how tall you are. He knows your thoughts and words even before you say them. You are created by God and he loves you very, very much!

READ OR LISTEN: Genesis 1:26-30 . Genesis 2:4-7

 Today, we will ...

THINK ABOUT...

What is your favorite thing God created?

Who is your favorite person and how would you describe them?
Why do you love them so much?

God's favorite part of creation is people, including YOU! What does that say
about who God is? What does that say about who you are?

What did you learn about God the Creator today?

Today, God did ...

P.S. PSALM 8 . ISAIAH 42:5 . ISAIAH 45:8-13

God's CHILDREN
Fearfully and Wonderfully Made

Psalm 139 gives us another picture of what it means to be created by God. He knew who you were, what you looked like, and the gifts you would have before you were born. He also knew all about the family you would be a part of. Do you want to know how? Because he made you. You are his work of art. You are his gift to the world.

This Psalm says the way God planned and designed us is like when someone weaves or knits (or paints or draws or builds) something beautiful. These words give us a picture of how carefully God planned us and designed us and made us.

We learned in Genesis that when God created people, he looked at everything he had made and said "very good." In these verses we learn that when God looks at YOU, he calls you amazing and wonderful. You are created by God. You are GOOD and AMAZING and WONDERFUL!

> *You made all the delicate, inner parts of my body*
> *and knit me together in my mother's womb.*
> *Thank you for making me so wonderfully complex!*
> *Your workmanship is marvelous - how well I know it.*
> **PSALM 139:13-14**

READ OR LISTEN: Psalm 139:1-14 .

Today, we will ...

THINK ABOUT...

Have you ever done something or made something that you were very proud of? Maybe a painting or a drawing. Or maybe you won a race or tried something new. What did you do or make and how did you feel?

Write or draw all the things God knows about you in the Psalm 139 passage. Did anything surprise you about what God knows about YOU?

What did you learn about being God's child today?

Today, God did ...

devo 12 God's CHILDREN
Our Heavenly Father

Calling someone Father or Dad means we are connected to them.

The same is true about God. We have a connection to God because he created us. You are God's child. That means you are one of his most beloved creations.

When we talk to God we can say the Lord's Prayer, or the Our Father. You might pray this at church or with your family at holidays or meals. The first words of the prayer are, "Our Father." In this prayer, God invites us to call him "our Father." Isn't that wonderful? We are each God's child.

We don't just have a heavenly Father. We also have many brothers and sisters. That's why the prayer says "OUR Father."

Our Father in heaven, may your name be kept holy.

May your Kingdom come and your will be done on earth as in heaven.

Give us daily bread, and help us forgive others as you forgive us.

Protect us from temptation and rescue us from the evil one.

READ OR LISTEN: John 1:12-13 . Matthew 6:9-13 .

Today, we will ...

THINK ABOUT...

Who is part of your family and what do you like about each person in your family? Draw a picture of your family here.

P.S.

READ JOHN 6:32-35 FOR ANOTHER IDEA ABOUT WHAT DAILY BREAD MIGHT MEAN. SEE DEVO 5.

If God is Father to ALL of us – how should we treat each other?

What did you learn about being God's child today?

Today, God did ...

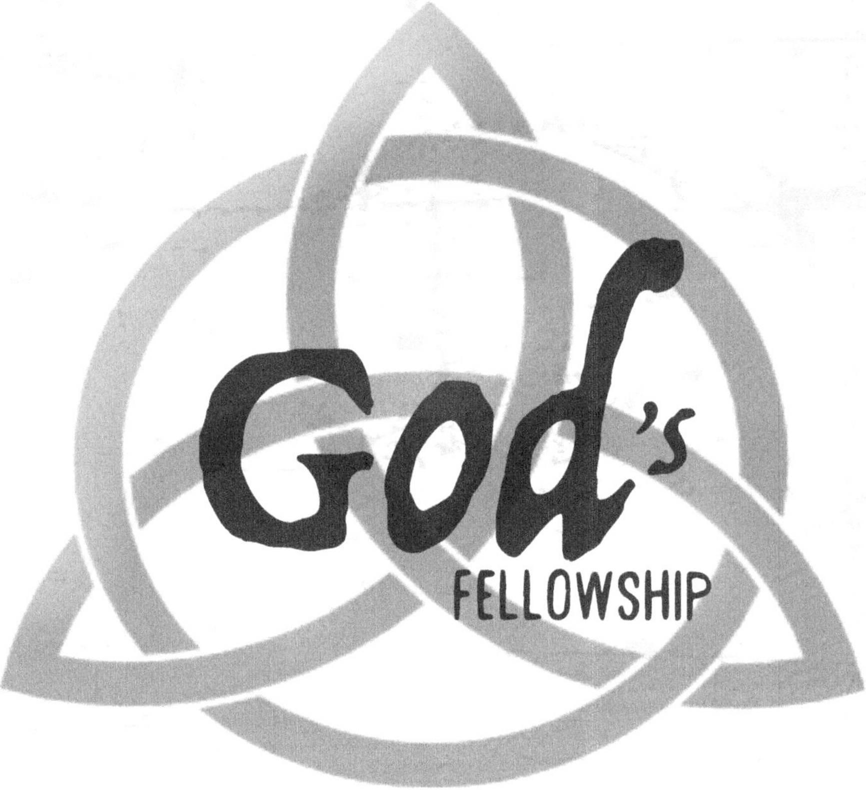

God's FELLOWSHIP

MAY THE GRACE OF THE LORD JESUS CHRIST, THE LOVE OF GOD,
AND THE FELLOWSHIP OF THE HOLY SPIRIT BE WITH YOU ALL.

2 CORINTHIANS 13:14

This section of **THREE-*in*-ONE** includes scripture passages that explain how God the Father, God the Son, God the Spirit, and God's children relate to and intersect with one another. Some of the earliest church teachers and leaders described the Trinity with a word that meant "to make space around." That word (*perichoresis*) is similar to the Greek word for "dance" (*choreuo*). The idea is that the Father, Son, and Spirit are engaged in a holy dance of love that leaves space around each other but also unites them as one. It's a beautiful metaphor and picture of God. As God's children, we are invited to join their dance of love. While living on this earth, we will never fully understand the dance or get all the steps right. But we can catch glimpses of it and can begin to experience it. Our God is **THREE-*in*-ONE.** He lives in the hearts of his children. His children live in him. This is indeed a holy mystery.

WE BELIEVE *in* GOD *the* FATHER,
ALMIGHTY MAKER *of* HEAVEN & EARTH.

WE BELIEVE *in* GOD *the* SON, JESUS CHRIST,
WHO DIED, ROSE, & REIGNS *from* HEAVEN.

WE BELIEVE *in* GOD *the* SPIRIT,
DWELLING IN & AMONG GOD'S PEOPLE.

WE BELIEVE *we are* GOD'S CHILDREN,
BELOVED *by the* FATHER, REDEEMED *by the* SON,
& EMPOWERED *by the* SPIRIT.

devo 13 God's FELLOWSHIP
A Rescue Story

Have you ever needed help from someone? Maybe you were not tall enough to reach the top shelf or maybe something was too heavy to carry alone or maybe something was difficult to understand.

We all need help. That is why it is good to live as families and communities. We don't have to figure out life alone, and so we can ask for help when we need it.

When sin first entered the world because of Adam and Eve's bad choice (that story in in Genesis 2 and 3), everything was affected and broken. God knew we would need help with that. That is why he sent his Son, Jesus, to the world.

God knew we could not fix ourselves. He knew we needed a helper to fix the brokenness in the world and to repair our relationship with God. It was a plan he had from the day brokenness and sin entered the world. God loves us way too much to not help us.

Now we can be rescued!

READ OR LISTEN: Romans 4:25-5:11

 Today, we will ...

THINK ABOUT...

What is something you need help with? Who is the first person you ask for help?

Who asks you for help sometimes? How do you help them?

When Jesus came to earth, what are some things he did to help us?

What did you learn about God today?

Today, God did ...

God's FELLOWSHIP
Mind Control

God the Son, Jesus, came to help us and rescue us from sin and brokenness. We need His help because we can not fix this brokenness alone. God had a plan for each of us so that we would be whole and know we belong.

Belong.

What a great word! Belonging means that we feel safe and wanted. God wants us to know when we say 'yes' to him - we belong. We are part of a big family - God's family. Each of us are wanted and needed and an important part of the family.

The most exciting thing about belonging to the family of God is this: there is nothing you can do to lose your belonging. Even when we make bad choices, we don't share, or when we are unkind, none of those choices kick us out of the family of God.

God says you belong. Today. Tomorrow. And forever.

You belong.

READ OR LISTEN: Romans 8:12-17

 *Today, we will ...*

THINK ABOUT...

Where is a place you love to go because you know that you belong there?
You could draw a picture of it here.

Who is a person that always makes you feel safe? How do they make you
feel safe? Do you feel those same feelings when you think about God?

What did you learn about God today?

Today, God did ...

God's FELLOWSHIP
Curse of Creation, Hope of the Spirit

When sin first entered the world because of Adam and Eve's bad choice, everything felt the consequences of sin. Things became broken.

It wasn't just people who felt the results of sin. Everything felt sin - even the ground and the water and the animals. Everything was broken.

Except God.

The good news is that God was not broken by sin. Someday all the brokenness, pain, and suffering in all of creation will be fixed and made right.

Until the day when God fixes all things and makes everything new, we can look to God every day and find his goodness and his love and his healing at work in our lives.

Even when all things feel broken and hard, God is with us now and will be with us every day. He can fix the broken things that happened in the past, the things that hurt today, and the things we worry about in the future.

READ OR LISTEN: Romans 8:19-30

 *Today, we will ...*

THINK ABOUT...

In what ways do we see the brokenness of creation? (hint: scary weather events or pollution or sad things in the world)

What is brokenness (sadness, sickness, etc.) you feel every day that you want God to fix?

What did you learn about God today?

Today, God did ...

devo 16 God's FELLOWSHIP
LOVE WINS!

Do you ever feel distant from someone who is right there beside you? You can see them and hear them - but for some reason they don't feel close in your heart or in your thoughts.

God is always with us - right beside us, inside of us, and all around us.

But sometimes it might not feel that way. Maybe because you are feeling sad about something. Maybe because you are going through a hard time. Maybe because you are thinking about something else and not paying attention to God.

The people who wrote the Bible knew that sometimes God's children might not feel close to him and might wonder if he really loves them. So they wrote some very important words to remind us that God is always there and that nothing can ever separate us from him or his love.

That is wonderful news! It means that no matter how we might feel, we can always know that God is there and that his love always lasts.

READ OR LISTEN: Romans 8:31-39

 Today, we will ...

THINK ABOUT...

Have you ever felt like God's love is far away? What happened?

What things might keep someone from remembering about God's love?

How can you remind yourself of God's love every day? Write some words here that will help you remember God's love.

Today, God did ...

devo 17 God's FELLOWSHIP
Living Sacrifice

One of the ways we say, "Thank you, God, for loving me so much," is to let him teach us how to live, how to think, and how to love people.

Another way we say, "Thank you, God, for loving me so much," is to work together with other people who love God and follow Jesus. The Bible says that when we do that, we are like a body.

Bodies have many parts - can you name some of them? - eyes, ears, nose, fingers, hands, and many more. Each of those parts does a special thing that only it can do. Eyes can't smell. Ears can't walk. Hands can't sing. Each part is special, and we need all of them.

God has something like a body, too, made of all his children. All of his children need each other, just like all of the parts of a real body need all the other parts. Each person who is part of God's body has a special job to do. No part is more important than any other part. God loves and uses every person.

Some of the different "parts" of God's body might be these: people who sing, people who teach, people who welcome others, people who help make things, people who help put things away, people who help with children, and people who do many other things

READ OR LISTEN: Romans 12:1-21

 Today, we will ...

THINK ABOUT...

What are some different things that people in "God's body" do?

What are the things that you do for "God's body"?

What things do your friends do for "God's body"? And your family?

 Today, God did ...

devo 18 — God's FELLOWSHIP
Rescued and Redeemed

Jesus is the one who rescues and saves us. He is the only one who can do that, because he is God. But God uses people to tell us and teach us about the very good story of Jesus and how we can be saved.

The book of Colossians is a letter that was written to real people a very long time ago. It was written with ink on special paper (not on a computer or phone), and it was delivered by hand (not by a postal worker). A man named Epaphras had told the Colossians (the people who lived in the city of Colossae) about the very good story of Jesus and how they could be saved. He taught them about Jesus and God and love and obedience and joy and kindness.

And then Epaphras told Paul - the man who wrote this letter - how kind and loving and faithful the people of Colossae were. So Paul wrote a letter to tell them, "Good job!"

Then he said, "But you must keep your faith steady and firm." Even when we are doing a very good job following Jesus and loving others, there are still ways we can grow and learn and love even more.

It is good to remember that following Jesus is wonderful, joyful, amazing, AND also hard work sometimes, especially on the days when we feel tired or grouchy or mad or selfish. Even on thoses days, remember God is still there, loving you!

READ OR LISTEN: Colossians 1:1-23

 *Today, we will ...*

THINK ABOUT...

Who teaches and tells you about Jesus?

What are some things that God would say, "Good job!" to you for.

What are some things that God would say, "But keep working hard at that."

Today, God did . . .

God's FELLOWSHIP
Jesus is Supreme

How would you describe Jesus to someone? What would you say about him?

You could tell some of the stories about him that are in the Bible.

You could talk about your experiences.

You could point at some of the things he created.

You could sing a song about him.

It's hard to describe how wonderful, wise, powerful, loving and kind Jesus is because he's SO MUCH and he's SO BIG and he's SO PERFECT.

One of the ways we can tell others about Jesus is by living the way he tells us to. Then people can see the love of Jesus in us.

How does your life show people what Jesus is like?

READ OR LISTEN: Colossians 1:15-20

Today, we will ...

THINK ABOUT...

What does "supreme" mean? (think about "supreme" pizza - biggest, best, everything)

How do you praise Jesus?

What thing about Jesus do you especially love?

What thing about Jesus do you think is especially amazing?

 Today, God did ...

devo 20 God's FELLOWSHIP
The Joy of Suffering

Usually, when people are facing troubles and problems, they don't rejoice. How do you respond to troubles and problems?

Some people complain. Some people get irritated. Some people get angry. Some people yell and cry and say, "It's not fair!"

Those feelings are real. And they make sense. But God doesn't want us to keep those feelings. He wants us to feel differently than what makes sense. His love and presence in our heart helps us with that.

Paul, the man who wrote today's verses, was in prison when he wrote. He had been put in prison because of his passionate and powerful preaching. He could have complained, or been irritated, or gotten angry, or yelled or cried and said, "It's not fair!"

But he wrote: "I am glad when I suffer for you in my body, for I am participating in the sufferings of Christ that continue for his body, the church." Paul said he was GLAD about what was happening to him because it was a result of his love and obedience to Jesus.

With Jesus' help, we can learn to be glad and rejoice even when we have troubles and problems.

READ OR LISTEN: Colossians 1:24-29, 2:1-5

Today, we will . . .

THINK ABOUT...

What troubles or problems do you have right now?

How do you feel about them? (you can list some words or draw a picture)

How can you begin to be glad and rejoice anyway?

What did you learn about who God is today?

Today, God did ...

devo **21** God's FELLOWSHIP
Keep On Keeping On

Have you ever started a new hobby or new book or new friendship that was very fun and exciting at first but then, after a while, not as much fun or as exciting? Sometimes we get tired of something because it's boring. Or because it's hard. Or because we don't like it as much as we did at first.

Jesus knows that people sometimes get bored or tired of things, not just hobbies or books or friends, but also following him. That's why the Bible reminds us that it's not enough to just accept Jesus or say "yes" to Jesus or to be excited about Jesus. Jesus wants his children to keep following him, to keep growing, to keep learning, to keep getting stronger, and to keep becoming more like him.

Think about a tree. When a tree starts growing, it doesn't stop after a few days or a few weeks or a few months and say, "I'm not going to grow anymore. This is as big as I'll get. I don't want any more leaves or branches. I'm tired of growing. I'll just stay the size I am." Trees keep growing deeper roots and stronger trunks and wider branches.

We can learn about following Jesus by looking at trees. When a tree has deep, strong roots, it grows stronger and taller every day. We will grow stronger if we have deep, strong roots in Jesus - not tree roots but faith roots (because you are a PERSON, not a TREE - but you are like a tree in some ways).

Every time you see a tree, think about growing deeper and stronger for Jesus.

READ OR LISTEN: Colossians 2:6-23

Today, we will ...

THINK ABOUT...

How do you help your body grow stronger?

How can you help your heart and your belief in Jesus grow stronger?

Draw a picture of a tree with deep roots, and YOU with deep roots.

 *Today, God did ...*

devo **22** # God's FELLOWSHIP
New Life, New People

How do you decide what clothes to wear each day?

You might think about these things:
> the weather (is it hot? cold? raining?)
> the events (is there a birthday? a party? a costume contest?)
> the place (are you going to school? to church? to work? camping?)

Each day we decide what clothes we will wear. We want clothes that fit us, serve a purpose, look a certain way, and are appropriate for what we'll be doing and where we'll be going.

Sometimes the Bible talks about our actions and attitudes like they are clothes. We should "take off" or "strip off" actions and attitudes that don't honor God or please Jesus. We should "put on" or "wear" actions and attitudes that show love to God and love to others.

In the morning when you decide what clothes you are going to wear, stop for a moment and think about what Jesus "clothes" you will wear, too - things like love, kindness, patience, forgiveness, and more.

READ OR LISTEN: Colossians 3:1-17

 *Today, we will ...*

THINK ABOUT...

What does the Bible say we should "strip off" or not wear?

What does the Bible say we should "put on" or wear? Draw a picture of you wearing those clothes.

How will you remember to wear those "clothes"?

Today, God did ...

devo 23   God's FELLOWSHIP
Listen and Live

One way to remember important things is to say them over and over again. Do you have things you say over and over again? Do you have other ways you try to remember things?

The person who wrote First John wanted people to remember important things about Jesus. So he talked about them over and over again.

> Jesus is God.
> Jesus is light.
> Jesus is love.
> We should love God and Jesus.
> We should love others.
> We should live in the light.
> We should obey God.
> Jesus is God.
> Jesus is light.
> Jesus is love.
> We should love God and Jesus.
> We should love others.
> We should live in the light.
> We should obey God.

Let's remember!

READ OR LISTEN: 1 John 1:1-10 and 1 John 2:1-17

 *Today, we will ...*

THINK ABOUT...

How do you know that Jesus loves you?

How is Jesus like light?

How will you remember these things about Jesus every day?

 Today, God did ...

God's FELLOWSHIP
Live in Light

Light and darkness are very different things. They are opposites.

One might make us feel happy and safe.

One might make us feel scared.

Sun makes us think of sun and warmth and daytime.

Darkness might make us think of nighttime and sleep, and maybe also fears of nightmares of feeling unsafe.

The book of 1 John says GOD IS LIGHT. Walking with God and living the way God asks us to is living in the LIGHT. 1 John also says that walking away from God and living our own way is living in DARKNESS. We can bring LIGHT or DARKNESS to the world depending on how we live. If we are kind, loving, caring, and generous, we bring the LIGHT of God to those around us. We can shine the LIGHT of God everywhere we go if we live for him!.

If we are unkind, unloving, selfish, or angry, we bring DARKNESS into the world. But when we realize this, we can ask God to forgive us. He always brings us back to the LIGHT.

READ OR LISTEN: 1 John 1:5-10 and 1 John 2:7-11

Today, we will ...

THINK ABOUT...

What do you think about when you think of LIGHT?

What feelings do you feel when you think about DARKNESS?

1 John describes God as LIGHT. What are other words you would use to describe who God is?

How can we live like God – as light – to others?

What can we do to show the light of God to others today?

What did you learn about God?

Today, God did ...

God's FELLOWSHIP
True Sons and Daughters

If someone asks you, "Who are you?" what would you say? Maybe you would tell them your name. Maybe you would tell them who your parents or siblings are. Maybe you would say you are a dancer or an artist or a basketball player.

All of these things are true about who you are and what makes you truly YOU.

If someone asks you, "Who is God?" what would you say? Maybe you would tell them that he made the world. Maybe you would tell them about your church. Maybe you would say that he is kind and good and loving.

All of these things are true about who God is.

The world has many wrong ideas about who God is and who you are. In fact, the world is full of lies about who God is and who you are. It's important to know the real truth so you can reject the lies.

Do you know what is especially true about you? You are a CHILD OF GOD. You are so deeply loved by God that he calls you HIS SON or HIS DAUGHTER. That's who YOU are! Next time someone asks you, "Who are you?" maybe your response could be, "I am a true child of the true God!"

READ OR LISTEN: 1 John 3:1-10

Today, we will ...

THINK ABOUT...

If someone asks you, "Who are you?" what are 5 different things you would tell them?

1.

2.

3.

4.

5.

What gifts has God given to YOU that makes you special or unique?

God calls you his SON or DAUGHTER. What does it mean to be a son or daughter?

What did you learn about God today?

Today, God did ...

devo **26** God's FELLOWSHIP
Real Love, False Prophets

God is LIGHT and we should live in it and share that LIGHT with others.

God is LOVE and we should live in it and share LOVE with others.

Before Jesus died on the cross, Jesus ate a final meal with his closest friends. One of the last things Jesus said to his friends was:

"I am giving you a new commandment:
Love each other. Just as I have loved you.
You should love each other. All your love
for one another will show the world that
you are my disciples." (John 13: 34-35)

Jesus said the world would know we are following him by the way we show LOVE to each other. When we LOVE we are also showing others who Jesus is.

When we LOVE others well, the LIGHT of Jesus shines through us to everyone we meet.

READ OR LISTEN: 1 John 4:7-20

 Today, we will ...

THINK ABOUT...

Who loves you well and how do they show you they love you?

What are ways we can show other people love? How do we show Jesus we love Him?

What did you learn about God today?

Today, God did ...

devo 27 God's FELLOWSHIP
Final Words, Final Warning

For the last few days we have read through the book of 1 John. We have remembered how much we are loved by God. We have learned that God is LIGHT. We heard God call us his SONS and DAUGHTERS. And we were reminded to LOVE each other.

In the last chapter of 1 John we are again reminded of all of those truths. (Parents and teachers remind us about important things, don't they? So does the Bible!)

But we are also given a warning to protect our hearts. It is a warning to keep away from DARKNESS and never put anything before God. In the last verse of the book of 1 John there is a warning, "Dear Children, keep away from statues of gods." (1 John 5:21) Another way to say that is:

> ## Dear children,
> ## keep away from anything that might take
> ## God's place in your hearts.

What an important reminder. Don't let anything take God's place in our hearts. Always put God first. When we put God first, we shine the LIGHT of God. We LOVE the way God calls us to love. And we remember we are CHILDREN OF GOD.

READ OR LISTEN: 1 John 5:1-21

 Today, we will ...

THINK ABOUT...

What is something you love (maybe a special gift or a picture) that you protect and keep safe?

How do you protect and guard things that are very important to you?

How can you guard and protect your heart, the special place where God lives with you?

What are things in your life that sometimes get more attention than God?

How do you keep God as your #1?

Today, God did ...

devo **28**

God's FELLOWSHIP
THREE-*in*-ONE (*in us as one*)

As followers of Jesus, we are always learning and seeking truth about

GOD THE FATHER
GOD THE SON
GOD THE SPIRIT

1. Because we love him and want to know him more.

2. Because we are called to live as LIGHT and LOVE.

3. Because the world is filled with DARKNESS. We must protect our hearts and minds.

We need to know about God and believe in God.
As followers of Jesus we also must remember who we are as

GOD'S CHILDREN

1. Because that is who we are.

2. Because we are called to live in LIGHT and LOVE.

3. Because the world is filled with DARKNESS . We must protect our hearts and minds.

We need to know who God says we are and believe it is true!
Look back and reflect on what you have read, heard, studied, and learned about God the Father, God the Son, and God the Spirit. Also, reflect on what it means to be a CHILD OF GOD.

READ OR LISTEN: Pick a favorite passage from the past month.

Today, we will ...

THINK ABOUT...

Think about what you have heard and learned about the three-in-one God and us, his beloved children. Write what you believe below.

This is who God the Father is:

This is who God the Son, Jesus is:

This is who God the Spirit is:

This is who God says I am:

 *Today, God did ...*

REMEMBER

Has there ever been a time when you looked around and thought: "I am never going to forget this moment?!" We hold tight to the great memories and big moments that change our life and bring us joy.

The Word of God is also something we are told to remember. We are told in the Bible to take the words of God and write them on our hearts so they are always near us. "Write them on our hearts" means that we remember God's words, hold onto them tightly, and then go back to them again and again so that we keep learning and never forget the truth about God.

Today we are going to spend some time remembering and reflecting on what we have read in the Bible and learned about God and ourselves.

PSALM 77:11
BUT THEN I RECALL ALL YOU HAVE DONE, O LORD. I REMEMBER YOUR WONDERFUL DEEDS OF LONG AGO. THEY ARE CONSTANTLY IN MY THOUGHTS. I CANNOT STOP THINKING ABOUT YOUR MIGHTY WORKS.

PSALM 103:1-2
I WILL PRAISE THE LORD.
DEEP DOWN INSIDE ME, I WILL PRAISE HIM.
I WILL PRAISE HIM BECAUSE HIS NAME IS HOLY.
I WILL PRAISE THE LORD.
I WON'T FORGET ANYTHING HE DOES FOR ME. (NIRV)

 Today, we will ...

THINK ABOUT...

Think back about what you have read, heard, and learned in this book.

Something I have learned about myself:

Something I have learned about God:

Something I have learned about my community or those who have done this with me:

 Today, God did ...

EXTRA THINGS

HERE'S A LIST OF SONGS, BOOKS, VIDEOS, AND OTHER CREATIVE THINGS THAT TELL THE TRUTH ABOUT WHO GOD IS AND WHO WE ARE.

SONGS & SPOKEN WORD:

KEITH & KRISTYN GETTY	"WE BELIEVE - APOSTLE'S CREED"
HILLSONG	"I BELIEVE"
HILLSONG	"SO WILL I (100 BILLION X)"
LECRAE	"IDENTITY"
LAUREN DAIGLE	"YOU SAY"
LAUREN DAIGLE	"LIGHT OF THE WORLD"
REND COLLECTIVE	"MY LIGHTHOUSE"
REND COLLECTIVE	"CHRIST LIVES IN ME"
AMENA BROWN	"HE IS HERE"
AMENA BROWN	"IN THE BEGINNING"
AMENA BROWN	"YOU"
ANDREW PETERSON	"IS HE WORTHY?"
ELLIE HOLCOMB	"WONDERFULLY MADE"
MATT MAHER	"BECAUSE HE LIVES"
MATT MAHER	"HOLD US TOGETHER"
MATT MAHER	"HOLY, HOLY, HOLY"
PROPAGANDA	"THE ONE AND ONLY JESUS"
TAUREN WELLS	"KNOWN"
TAUREN WELLS	"CITIZEN OF HEAVEN"
TRANSMISSION	"THREE IN ONE"
TRANSMISSION	"JESUS SON OF GOD"
TRANSMISSION	"FALLEN, BROKEN"
TRANSMISSION	"LOVE WINS"

**The full album by transMission can be found at www.ussmusicandarts/org/we-believe
All songs are based on the Creeds.

EXTRA THINGS (CONT'D)

BOOKS:

BASIC CHRISTIANITY	JOHN STOTT
CORE CHRISTIANITY	MICHAEL HORTON
MERE CHRISTIANITY	C. S. LEWIS

AUDIO BIBLE:

STREETLIGHTS BIBLE APP (STREETLIGHTS.COM)
AUDIO OF FULL NEW TESTAMENT (NLT) WITH HIP HOP SOUNDTRACK

VIDEOS:

BIBLE PROJECT (BIBLEPROJECT.COM) "THEMES" SERIES

GOD
HOLY SPIRIT
THE MESSIAH
IMAGE OF GOD

BIBLE PROJECT "HOW TO READ THE BIBLE" SERIES

VIDEOS + BIBLE STUDY + DEVO:

LEARN IMPORTANT STUFF ABOUT GOD
AND JESUS AT THIS SITE WHICH HAS
BIBLE PROJECT VIDEOS + YOUNG LIFE STUDIES:

(BIBLEPROJECT.COM/PARTNER/YOUNG-LIFE)

BIBLE READING PLANS:

USE THIS QR CODE TO DOWNLOAD
THE BIBLE APP'S YOUNG LIFE HOMEPAGE
FOR A SERIES OF BIBLE READING PLANS
WITH DAILY DEVOS.

DAILY MINI-DEVOS:

@YL_DISCIPLESHIP ON INSTAGRAM

MORE EXTRA THINGS

AUTHORS, ARTISTS, QUOTES, SONGS, BOOKS, VIDEOS, AND OTHER RESOURCES
THAT YOUR FRIENDS & LEADERS RECOMMEND:

WE BELIEVE *in* GOD *the* FATHER,
ALMIGHTY MAKER *of* HEAVEN & EARTH.

WE BELIEVE *in* GOD *the* SON, JESUS CHRIST,
WHO DIED, ROSE, & REIGNS *from* HEAVEN.

WE BELIEVE *in* GOD *the* SPIRIT,
DWELLING IN & AMONG GOD'S PEOPLE.

WE BELIEVE *we are* GOD'S CHILDREN,
BELOVED *by the* FATHER,
REDEEMED *by the* SON,
& EMPOWERED *by the* SPIRIT.

22962479R00064